OUR OBSIDIAN TONGUES

DAVID SHOOK

OUR OBSIDIAN TONGUES

For Robert
& for Claire,
who makes the
best faces in
the audience!
Thanks!

25 Apr. 13

EYEWEAR PUBLISHING

First published in 2013
by Eyewear Publishing Ltd
74 Leith Mansions, Grantully Road
London W9 1LJ
United Kingdom

Typeset with graphic design by Edwin Smet
Author photograph by Travis Elborough
Printed in England by TJ International Ltd, Padstow, Cornwall

ISBN 978-1-908998-07-1

WWW.EYEWEARPUBLISHING.COM

David Shook studied endangered languages in Oklahoma and poetry at Oxford. His many translations include Roberto Bolaño's Infrarealist manifesto, Mario Bellatin's novellas, and Víctor Terán's poetry from the Isthmus Zapotec. He served as Translator in Residence for the Poetry Parnassus, where he premiered his poetry documentary *Kilómetro Cero*, covertly filmed in Equatorial Guinea. Shook grew up in Mexico City, but now lives in Los Angeles, where he edits *Molossus* and Phoneme Books.

Table of Contents

Nimitstlasotla nosiwaw.

This is the city and I am one of the citizens,
Whatever interests the rest interests me....

Walt Whitman

Our Obsidian Tongues

after Tecuani

Our tongues are neither spoons
nor arrows. Neither flower petals
nor leaves. Our tongues are
obsidian tongues, shorter than
the knives priests use to sacrifice
but equally sharp. Our tongues
flint sparks. Our tongues chip
thin flakes when stabs
aren't straight & quick. Our
tongues are neither spoons
nor arrows, petals nor leaves.
Our obsidian tongues.

The last few months I've looked on her with pity.
I'm on the tenth floor & even here I hear the whines
of drills, the rumor of automobiles &
the whimpering of dogs that refuse to die.

I observe her intensely, I try to see the sun through her haze. At such
an early hour the city is a yawning pachyderm.

My father had a vision
through the double-window of an airplane:

Aztec gods protecting their city, arms folded
like celestial bouncers.

Their listless kids swim, jump cannonballs
into sulphuric lakes, tickle volcanoes

until they laugh ash. At night they get high huffing
bus fumes, pheromones & sweat.

The sun rises each morning without human sacrifice.
The misery of the city is enough.

In the neonatal ward of the hospital
a thousand rabid infants,
tiny tongues dense with thrush

Silvestre Adán

as carpenter

I hewed six pews from the pine logs we netted in the Balsas,
chiseled the wind into the robes of the saints in San Miguel,

carved lips & brows, hollowed nostrils. Sawed soft wood
into tables, sanded moisture from its skin. Seldom chairs.

Boxes for the dead, when boxes. Like Jorge's son:
body bloated with the river's spit, eyes glazed with mezcal.

I still doctor the stubbed toes of Santiago,
massage Juan Bautista's cracked palms with heated sap.

Rub ash from their singed feet,
admire joints hinged tighter than my own.

The newspapers say you're two packs a day

flavored like souvenir cigars: bus exhaust, fruit rot,
soured smoke of boiling hops, trash & burnt plastic

limited edition ash fall

[Best Western Weslaco pool scene, postmarked Weslaco, Texas, 19 July 1998, addressed to Lupe Peña de Hiriart, Av. Miguel Hidalgo 56, Granjas Lomas de Guadalupe, 54760 Cuautitlan Izcalli, Edo. Mexico]

You know how this begins: after two days
they demand more money than we agreed on,
& what can we do, right? We're out in the
desert in a town made of tents, cinder
blocks & semi-trucks. We're thinking of ways
to find cash, cause they put what we eat on
a tab too. Even though you did what we
told you, like my wife did what we told her,
they still wanted more. He was vomiting
by then, thin pink strings that striped the sand
outside our plastic tarp. He heaved at night.
I told him we should wait it out, till something
changed—& I shouldn't have let him demand
we leave. I'll just say it. Your husband died.

At the Baptist Seminary Dormitories in Mexico State

Earwigs drown in shared sinks, whirlpool down the drains
of cement showers splotched with paint by teams of

teens & chaperones descended from their heaven to roll more
coats on walls inches thick with sloppy layers of lead-free.

Silverfish mate beneath the seminary pillows like sequins fucking.
One boy waits through the tuning half-snores, sighs &

rolling readjustments of his roommates until their chorus joins
            the crickets,
night trucks, the hall's fluorescent buzz. Soundtrack to

his dull & guilty masturbation. Week's end he'll leave his shoes &
most shirts to practice sacrifice,

save one, bunched between his wool poncho & dopp kit,
strings of dead semen starched like sweat.

A wasp hive hangs from the chapel awning, papered tombs'
doors rolled back to reveal their peanut shell interiors, empty.

I Know Your Body

after Víctor Terán

If you were a city
I could give perfect directions
to wherever they asked me,
I could map your neighborhoods &
catalogue your smells.

If you were a city
I would get lost every day
down some new corridor.
I would toss my map, hitchhike
your suburbs, wander your downtown.

The Needle

Its ancestors were tiny slivers of flint with bare shoulder blades for eyes. Bird bones, fish ribs, thin thorns. Some species of cacti have the appropriate spine morphology, especially members of the padded family Opuntia: Beavertail, Teddybear Chola, Woolyjoint & others. Its eye an anus (shitting string?) or the whale's eye of a dick, the so short and so narrow hallway through which each bloody string of the quartered camel must be drawn, for the rich man, with his soiled apron, to approach the gate of heaven. Bushwacker, trailblazer, tiny wormhead burrowing through felt, leather, cloth. A virgin pole of Western Red Cedar, eager for the thousand faces of an Ojibwe totem, frozen over. Slenderest of icicles. Bakhtin's white gold toothpick, the only luxury he afforded himself in Kustanai. Robotic eyelash. Lowercase L sans serif. John Cage's tiny baton in the diorama of *4'33"* at the Tehran Museum of Music, funded by the generosity of patron Empress Pahlavi, who attached to her gift two simple stipulations: that that diorama be featured in the great entry hall of the museum where her bust might otherwise reside & that Monsieur Cage's baton be made of the needle her nursemaid used to patch her childhood gowns. The needle speaks a tiny language, inaudible, even, to music box prongs & harmonica reeds & dentists' vibrating scrapers of plaque. Tinier than Polish.

The city smells bad. With spring
the sewers have bloomed. Through the dust & ozone,
jacarandas flash, swords of color & the penetrating stench
of rotten oranges.

My tongue is a rudder like a trout fin
swimming in

the volcanic dregs of a shrinking lake
so opaque

that only the fin itself can know
which direction the fish will go.

In the retirement homes, spare rooms,
hospice, thrush blooms stealthily like mold,
like cobwebs over tongues too seldom moved

Praise Song for Santiago Matamoros

after Moisés Náufrago

I praise you for knowing us from Moors,
for recognizing our skin not as their desert leather,
our hearts not as their small stones, like the pits of
dates or apricots.

I praise you for your wooden ears.
They do not ring through our hourly barrage of
rockets, buzz of sparklers beneath your
concrete dome.

I praise you for mezcal, tequila, beer,
unnamed liquors in their faded plastic two-liters.

I praise you for revenge, for mosquitos' palate for
imported blood, for dengue, malaria, E. coli, some cholera.

For guilt.

I praise you for the dam they couldn't build.

For the cattle-killers whose black tails
lick the ankles of thieves, know their prey by
scent & heart alone.

I praise you for mezcal, again.

I praise you, Santiago Matamoros,
Santiago Mataindios, Black Santiago on
your cloudy horse.

Silvestre Adán

as farmer

I've thumbed a thousand seeds into their
nests, I've asked them to grow tall as men.
Come chili. Come corn, come watercress.
Come plum and mango from your trees.
My knees are rough as cinder. My fingers
know the life of worms. I am a fish gone slack in
the net, tired of the river's silty tricks. Come sleep.

You hide the city like
asterisks hide the *us* & *is* of
   *fuck*s & *shit*s

like string bikinis cover nipples

a sheet-draped mass on the highway shoulder

Blood is only blood when warm, when
cold it congeals to simple mess,
to a nightly shift & a thin
wad of cash to wire back. I dress
in the same stained jeans each night, the was-blood
& soapy water soak through to my thighs.
The butcher's apron is prop. Soured cud
& matted hair leave on my shoes. Guys
like me are a dime a dozen
so I can't complain: it's work &
work is money. Lately I've been
doing doubles, since Luis got canned.

Work's in our blood—in blood—you used to say.

My love to Chueco, Maria, José—

Offerings to Tule

1

Through the branches
light stripes its thumbtip horns.
The dome of its skull is the base of
a pitcher retching its gelatinous dregs
at the speed of sap. Blood drips from
the neck. The ants that live along
the roots circle drops like roundabouts.
The priest will leave it hanging till
its eyes dry, till its lids cave like
a womb postpartum.

2

Over a thin branch, xylem still pliable, a pair
of small shoes hang tied by their laces like a
phone wire taunt in miniature. Their feet turn
to dirt inside wool socks, in the earth beneath Tlalixtac.

3

A trumpet like an artificial limb,
a brass or copper branch, the mouth of
a tree that after two-thousand years
has not yet evolved to speech.

The Rest of the Cow

Its body in the butcher shop, its
tongue, too. Its mouth an empty
home papered in cud.
The butcher's dog will eat
its heart, relish its saltiness, the
heart that beat like a trout
fresh on the floor of a boat
as the knife approached its neck.
Which of its seven stomachs
tensed first, which will make
the least bitter stew?

Below there are policemen, shoe shines, nurses, dwarves, muggers.
Flames leap from windows & the sirens' shriek proclaims
the lordship of violence.

Here on the tenth floor we dead walk with suspicion, distressed,
alert, they won't kill us again.

In the glass & rebar phalluses that house
commerce, industry & glossy magazines
a banker examines his tongue in a bathroom
mirror: wrapped in a blanket of ghostflesh,
yellowish, gauzelike, Casper's tongue

A Portrait of the Question Mark

Graphologists have studied it for centuries: it grows upside down like hanging tomatoes—but from a tiny bulb of period—into a woman pregnant with wonder or frustration. Its mirror ends questions: postpartum food-baskets, temptation for man & child alike. English speakers, obsessed with breasts, have forgotten the womb that makes them swell & abandoned the expectant mother of the question.

Silvestre Adán

as artist

A dozen works by forty watts
each night till I lost my eyes,
one at a time. Rolled eighty
paintings each week & mailed
them to the beach. Went myself
to paint memories on shirts &
hats. My cousin still whines, derides
the shots & tits of cheap tourist shit.
Tits belong to cows, I tell him, Talk milk
or talk nice. Women liked my rabbits,
mid-leap. Men scorpions, teeth.

Smog flags like riptide warnings at the beach:
stay indoors if red, walk if orange, light sports if
yellow, if green fine

never green

[Promotional business postcard for Inglés QuickLearning, slogan "¡Para que no te dan la cara de *what*!" postmarked Nicolás Romero, Mexico State, 30 April 2007, addressed to Casa Johnson, Avenida Centenario 2699-A, Casa 11, 01590 Mexico D.F.]

We don't want much & I think it's fair
because it's probably my family
that sweat & broke their backs for that money
anyway. I don't pretend that we are
Robin Hoods or Zapatistas. I'm not
kidding myself into thinking I'm in
the right—I carved his ear off, cleaned his skin
with my own tequila. I haven't shot
him yet. This shit doesn't make me any
happier than it does you guys. I swear
I cringe at his bare tragus. The kid wears
it like a nipple on his swollen face—   Many
wouldn't last this long. Eighty thousand by
Monday or he's dead. Look:

Don't let me die.

Peluqueria Poema

He attacks Mother Nature for a small fee.

There is a carpet here of hair.
There is a heaven of curled clouds.
Lice praise me with their harps.

Neck, this is breeze. Breeze, neck.
I introduce cheekbones to sun,
I hide roots' climb towards light.

I've heard hair keeps growing after death,
but I've never styled a corpse. I fight years
with dye & foil, sweep the evidence away.

If some god knows how many hairs
we each have, I write his riddles with
my scissors.

for The Hive Los Angeles

Sacrificing Chickens to the Lake Before Corn Season

Tie a brick to the chicken's neck with twine.
Ankle, wire, rock. The lake doesn't care.

I like to watch their wings' last flaps, their
feathers come loose. I like to hold my breath.

Last year the neighbor's rooster ripped off
its yellow claw, let it sink with its cinder block
anklet, knot tied tighter than tendon.

Its blood pooled flat across the lake, broken by
the bubbles of the cinder's secret air.

We stoned & bricked the bird until it sank.
I clocked its beak off with a spinning rock
but it wouldn't shut up, kept squawking
the chorus of the thousand poultry ghosts
beneath the water: chicken skeletons, eyes picked
by fish, hens' bones bleached plaster white,
cocks perched on their chance tombstones, waiting.

First the yellow foot, eventually the bird.

The flat roofs are elevated patios, cat nests, hospice for the flowerpots.
Sheets, tablecloths, & straitjackets fade in cages. The wind dead,
a beer billboard sags. A granny swats at
invisible wasps. A cyclist remembers mornings when the volcanoes
were visible, he is distracted & a taxi splits his ribs.

Four Ash Fall Questions

1. The Vulcanologist

Hasn't ashed like this since Kennedy's visit in '62,
an army of tephra stretched across the polluted sky,

soldiers of coarse & fine ash, lapilli sergeants &
agglomerate commanders linger behind their troops.

Popocatépetl's ash cone swells, the city is too busy
for tuff to cement. The pale yellow of early ashfall grays,

the city is perfumed with sulphur. All flights suspended,
air tense with tephric static. Asthmatic children

cough in chorus, smokers smoke inside.
Will tomorrow bring your Bishop's ring?

2. The Nurse

If your throat is the cone that ends in
your rocky lips, your intestines have been

swollen deep within the earth for days.

Lava burns your oesophagus. You vomit rocks.
Who will wipe the filth from your lips?

3. The Mango Vendor

The streets are salted with ash
like the first day of each new year,

without the newspaper skins of
fireworks. The boys

with their bottles & rags do
so good their pockets clink.

Mangos sell like normal, no
tabloid gossip here no rush.

Two for one today, swollen with
real rain. Why not try, why not

bite into the only reds & oranges
not dulled by ash?

4. Boy in Alvaro Obregon

The sun burns orange through
the haze, the color of ripe peach

flesh near its pit, bar flash
neon, the glow of heated

metal, the lit tip of god's cigarette.
When will you lift it from

the ashtray of the valley?

Silvestre Adán

as orchard keeper

I feed the throat hum
of my suck-pump with
a half can of
lead-free each day till
melons swell with promise &
you can smell the river on
husks of corn two heads
taller than a man.

Evenings I feed the dogs,
sharpen my machete,
then hang in my hammock,
listen for rabbits & kids.
Mornings I swim across the
Balsas, wet my hair & pray for
rain, praise for watermelon.

earwax gray,
mucus marbled black

[Polaroid of unidentified man, smiling in a makeshift soccer uniform, stamped and postmarked Weslaco, Texas, 4 January 1999, addressed to Lupe Peña de Hiriart, Av. Miguel Hidalgo 56, Granjas Lomas de Guadalupe, 54760 Cuautitlan Izcalli, Edo. Mexico | written in white margin of photograph]

Dear Lupe,
please forgive me—
nothing to say—
my last letter
was a lie:
your husband, he
didn't really die.
You're better
off, though you
won't believe
it yet. Do
the kids know?
Let em grieve
a dead hero.

There are more parabolic antennas than trees. Small buzzards, very similar to doves, fly over the streets in search of crumbs or
       excrement.
Gas cylinders crack into life. Plastic cisterns' rooftop mouths are dry & wait, trembling, for the acid rain of rainy season.

Mutt Ghazal

They loiter like teenagers with time to kill before curfew.
        Every chilango dog
the same, they inspect the sidewalk for dropped pork skin, lime rinds—
        here a slow dog

is a thin one. With corporate sponsorship and a haircut I could host
        The World's Ugliest
Dog Pageant—two-to-one odds on the ochre pooch at the bus stop.
        A real show dog,

her lipstick nipples hang from sucked-empty sacks. Runner-up might
        go to
the chihuahua mix with hail damage & no insurance. & so dog

after dog they parade the sidewalk. The ribskinny pit with
        premature mange
& the three-legged shepherd mutt will fight for third, after the break.
        No dog

will win Congeniality, they're all bitches here. They represent adjectives
        instead of
states: Misses Neck-Nipping, Snarling, Teethless, Maybe Rabid—
        whoa, dog—

The pit beats tripod to a dropped tortilla, cares more about dinner than
the contents of the winner's envelope. Listen, quid pro quo, dog,

you wanna win? David's the same as you. He spends his day
        loitering online,
scribbling poems. Forget world peace—money is the way to go, dog.

A woman with thrush tongue-kisses
a man with~~out~~ thrush

The Toothpick

The most democratic of mouth furniture, health benefits of the periodontal variety confirmed & only rumors of stomach splinters afflicting heavy chewers. What tiny woodsmith can hew a toothpick? What carpenter possesses the concentration required for the carving of a perfect wooden obelisk? What anorexic earthworm could dig a posthole small enough not to swallow it whole? A telephone pole in renewable birch, a fencepost for the sparrow's nest, prehistoric diorama spear, punt-pusher in a shallow pint of milk. Friar Norbello decried, in perfect octosyllable, that the Wise Men from the East hadn't brought the Christ-child toothpicks: even the pre-plaque from that holy mouth might one day make a relic. Eskimos would use a thin reed of baleen, a habit the whalers on Deception Island learned for lack of wood. In 1862 the first plastic toothpick was presented, by Alexander Parkes, at the Great International Exhibition in London. The Eames' most famous fight was fought over the color of the toothpicks to be displayed on their Case Study dining table (Ray: yellow; Charles: red).

Silvestre Adán

as morning singer

Come chili. Come corn, come watercress.
Come plum and mango from your trees.

[Postcard of Acapulco cliff divers at sunset, in midair, postmarked Acapulco, Guerrero, 18 May 1997, addressed to Familia Hernández, Calle Troya #168, Colonia Lomas de Axomiatla, 01820 Mexico D.F.]

Weather's great! Just over 30°.

Yes, I drank too many young coconuts—
Sarah warned me the milk would steep through my
weak intestines, released as fecal tea—
an image you might like. Our new friend cuts
their green skins off with his machete. Buy
one cold for one peso more & he'll dig
it from the foam ice chest where they're nestled
like coir-coated ostrich eggs or mini
bowling balls. At home they're never this big.

This evening we saw a boy wrestle
a gull to the sand. He held its wings, free
to fly at arm's length like a toy plane. Each
shoulder snapped. He blessed his meal, walked the beach.

the sky over the city like a
tongue cream with thrush

The Pin

after Hugo Hiriart

Skeleton? No, ascetic body & investigative spirit; its head theologically populated by angels and its straight & solemn metallic meat mortified. The beautiful Melisanda hid venomous pins amidst her long hairs, painted yellow; mimicry is appropriate (also the symbol of the serpent that hides in the flowers): hairs, pins, needles (the workers that sew, the bourgeois that weave, the delinquents that inject), barbs, pointers, teeth (from combs & some fish), spines, bones, feet & antennae of insects, wires (transmitters & fuses), foils belong to the same family, they're complicit, pimps & fences for each other. Among the questions raised we can formulate: which delicate and precise door has the needle as its only key? What strong man could punch it? Against whom would he fight, the knight who confers the pin its precious point? How much prodigious mating will we conceive of if we take the pin to have a phallic quality? What language are these subtle practices of Kama Sutra written in? Is there a known Chinese monarch whose sceptre was a pin? Has the art of pin decorators been lost forever? What diminutive mammal brandishes them like antlers? But, let's leave the questions. The master tattooist looks lovingly on his wise pins, to his right extends the white and trembling back of the girl on whom he will engender the carnivorous spider that will devour her; fulfilling his ancient honor as artist, Tanizaki Junichiro applies himself with great care to the task, & the girl crosses her eyes in pleasure. The acupuncturist sits beside his convulsed, anxious & chubby pincushion & decides to begin with the open hand. Let's leave spindles & incidents with pins behind, we won't talk any more about undertakers making tombs of pins or the Norman warrior who split pins longitudinally with a single saber swipe, we will observe the pin alone & isolated: what is it? It's a monument, a Giacometti meditator, a Brancusi statue, a perfect obelisk erected in the forest.

The phone won't stop ringing. Others call us from
distant vertical cemeteries.
Everything outside is gray. Here on the tenth floor, no color
but the lipsticked lips of the preteen dead.

I peer down again to admire the spring.

Surrounded by trash lovers kiss & rats mate.

Postcard from Los Angeles

Sometimes I trick myself into thinking
that I'm back. In Echo Park it's easy:
kids play in Spanish, a man in a coat
sells corn with butter, mayonnaise, & chili.
He's always in his coat. Weekends he'll bring
homemade popsicles sheathed in plastic; we
like mandarin the best, it makes your throat
itch in a good way. You know the story
about the fake cigarettes I bought in
Chapultepec, with the powder smoke? Here
it's like I'm in some corner of that park,
showing her around. We're lost but fine. When
we walk back home I blow my nose to clear
the city's debris. But my mucus isn't dark

Fourth Tenochtitlan

after Eduardo Lizalde

Over the howling valley of
some god's throat: breath
warm & rank   high-hopped
beer & grain alcohol in plastic
bottles by night   burnt coffee
& diesel by morning   & nothing
but the dry mouth of hunger
during the day

★

Its nebulas of insects
DEET-proof beasts with
beaks   & wings thicker
than glass   no eyelash
hairs for legs   no pinpoint
eyes   nebulas, galaxies of
beetles   a colony of roaches
in the cast-iron stove

★

A continent of downy aeronauts
floats over the city   the tectonic
city shifts like an uneasy plate
jostling its neighbors for space
but the down for all its fluff
weighs more than lead   but the
down sticks to the city like cement

★

The green eyes of a monstrous
butcher guard the edges of the
sinkhole   his cleaver is dull but
still he uses it with vigor   he chops
with squawk & flame like a gunshot
like he's stalking the bovine corpses
from a deerstand   & he is silent with
his mouth

⋆

A plane passes by   at night they're
like jewels on an invisible string
descending into protracted
numbness   the hollow laughter
of old friends   the boys that
gargle gasoline on corners
to make a meal's worth of change

⋆

The condors have their cage
barred with volcanic peaks
they feed themselves the carrion
that litters the streets: dog meat,
goat meat, chickens & hares
sacrificed to the rich   to the
tires of cars   discarded

Police helicopters scramble dinner sitcoms. Pharmacists
run out of condoms, no back stock. Even novelty gloves, gone.
The faded photo-cells of solar panels will work as sepia mirrors.

The poets are stoned & lonely or lonely & stoned
& maybe thrush was once a bird.

Incense

after Tecuani

My tongue is a bundle of sage, O
My tongue is a bundle of sage, O
Wild sage, picked from the foothills
Where bees nest after their toil
With the flowers, where bees
Nest after their dances & feasts
My tongue is a bundle of sage, O
Burning like incense from its tip

Notes

'The Degradation of Spring' begins as a version of Francisco Hernández's poem of the same name, then evolves into my own.

'Like Asterisks' has an accompanying score written by violist Adrian Wong.

'Fourth Tenochtitlan' uses my lines of Eduardo Lizalde's 'Third Tenochtitlan' to begin each strophe.

look what I planted today —he told her—
cactus & euphorb & succulents for you,
sand for me, words & worms for you, a pebble
or what do I have here? glass! a drop of blood,
Bee, my blood for you.

Acknowledgements

Thanks to the editors of *Ambit*, *Anomalous Press*, *Debacle*, *Maple Tree Literary Supplement*, *Oxonian Review*, *Poetry London*, *Wasafiri*, & *World Literature Today*, where versions of some of these poems & their contemporaries found early homes. Thanks to the editors of *Wasafiri*, who nominated 'Mutt Ghazal' for the 2012 Forward Prize. Thanks too to the editors of the anthologies *Oxford Poets 2010* (Carcanet) & *Initiate: New Oxford Writing* (Blackwell) for their publication of versions of some of these poems. Thanks to Sarah Maguire at the Poetry Translation Centre for commissioning my translations of Víctor Terán.

Thanks to Syd & Okie Doke: I love you; to Mom, Dad, Sarah, Ashley, & Biscuit, for being there in Mexico City; to my Nahuatl family the Adáns; to the Mexican poets I've cannibalized here: Francisco Hernández, Hugo Hiriart, Eduardo Lizalde, Tedi López Mills, Moisés Naúfrago, Víctor Terán, & Tecuani; to my Oxford teachers Jenny Lewis & Jamie McKendrick; to all those who have supported this book with their generous recommendations: Philip Gross, David Huerta, Sudeep Sen, Daniel Simon; to all my friends & collaborators around the world.

EYEWEAR POETS

MORGAN HARLOW MIDWEST RITUAL BURNING
KATE NOAKES CAPE TOWN
RICHARD LAMBERT NIGHT JOURNEY
SIMON JARVIS EIGHTEEN POEMS
ELSPETH SMITH DANGEROUS CAKES
CALEB KLACES BOTTLED AIR
GEORGE ELLIOTT CLARKE ILLICIT SONNETS
HANS VAN DE WAARSENBURG THE PAST IS NEVER DEAD
DAVID SHOOK OUR OBSIDIAN TONGUES